AF255806

More Than Words

More Than Words

MARTIN BROADBELT

RESOURCE *Publications* · Eugene, Oregon

MORE THAN WORDS

Resource Publications
An Imprint of Wipf and Stock Publishers
199 W. 8th Ave., Suite 3
Eugene, OR 97401

www.wipfandstock.com

PAPERBACK ISBN: 978-1-6667-6424-6
HARDCOVER ISBN: 978-1-6667-6425-3
EBOOK ISBN: 978-1-6667-6426-0

VERSION NUMBER 030723

Contents

The Hand You're Dealt

ME AGAINST SOCIETY

I lye within the belly of the beast,
Searching for salvation,
Escaping reality,
With the hopes of being embraced by serenity.
　　　But, society emerges his ugly head,
　　　Awakening the mislead.
Corrupting the fortunate,
And disrupting the innocent.
　　　I find myself lost within it,
　　　Erupting with untamed temptations,
　　　I desire the celebration of my own emancipation.
But, I'm blindsided by the foolishness of common sense,
And manipulated at my expense.
For trying to bring attention,
To the nonsense.
　　　It's hopeless to assume things will get better,
　　　When those appointed,
　　　Are unconcerned,
　　　With trying to shelter us from bad weather.
So, here I stand,
Just a man,
That society has left alone,
To suffer the storm on his own.

SINGLE MOTHER

Working from 9 to 5,
Was never enough to survive.
       So, you work first and third shift,
       Never pitching a fit,
       Over sleep being missed.
Living each day as difficult as the next,
Trying not to come submerged in life's stress.
You give it your best,
Only focusing on the positive,
And saying, fuck you to all the rest.
       Money is always an issue,
       With bills striking like heat seeking missiles,
Giving you nowhere to run or hide,
So, you close your eyes.
Looking forward to the morning after,
Forgetting the destruction of your economic disaster.
       Even though at times it all seems hopeless,
       You never lose focus.
Always getting the job done,
Reassuring a future for your daughter and son.
But times are hard,
And the light at the end of the tunnel,
Seems so far.
       Society demands are tough,
       And giving it your all just isn't enough.
Disappointment pulls you close to the edge,
And thoughts of giving up begin to fill your head.
But being the strong woman you are,
You take off, like a shooting star.
       Blasting through the miseries of the dark,
       Ripping the sounds of negativity apart.

Struggling to keep a hold on your sanity,
You find strength from the intimacy of your family.
> Even though a higher learning passed you by,
> There was never an outcry,
> For a reason why,
> When raising your firstborn became your life.
And now what a woman you've become,
Similar to many,
But identical to none.
> You are an inspiration of life,
> Shining your light,
> On all single mothers,
> Trying to find their way through the night.

CHICAGO TIMES

On my corner, streets are hard,
Gangsters, drug dealers, and pimps,
Create a setting for the misfortunate and the starved,
While men stagger around with active battle scars,
And life expectancy weighs in at a staggering 24,
If you plan on surviving,
You must commit,
And be willing to solicit,
A hiccupping fire spitting persuader,
To influence the hater's,
Cause talk comes cheap,
And those who speak with words,
Are preserved,
Where the disregarded undyingly sleeps,

On my corner, the crazy, the homeless, and the walking dead fill
my streets,
And the pimps, gangsters, and drug dealers,
Provide me with money for clothes and food to eat.
You must understand,
In my house there was no man,
So, I became a welcoming witness,
To their existence,
Unconcerned with they're wrongs
They made me feel like I belonged,
And a partnership was created,
Between the rejected and the hated,
And with this treaty,
They found redemption,
And I, acceptance,

On my corner, single mothers are used and abused,
Exhausted to a point to where they're confused.
Doing everything they can,
But with just two hands,
They cannot meet life's demands.
Struggling just to keep food on the table and roof over everyone's
head,
Stressful times make them consider life would be better if they
were dead,
While a river of tears floods their eyes,
They kneel praying at the foot of their beds.

On my corner, fathers abandon their families,
For life on the streets,
Living on corners and in alleys.
While the ones' that stay,
Find it hard to make a way.
Working 3 and 4 jobs at a time,
Just to make ends meat,
And still unable to eat.
Going days without sleep,
You worry from week to week,
Drained to a point of almost defeat.

On my corner, it is hopeless to try and find,
A day full of sunshine,
During these Chicago times.

A FATHER MISSIN

Being picked on and called names,
Came close to driving me insane,
So, I walked side by side with frowns,
And ran from smiles.
       Surviving predicaments,
       That begged for your guiding hand,
       I search endlessly for answers,
       When I question being a man,
              Leaving me no choice,
              But to deal on my own,
              The concrete jungle took me in,
              And society's streets became my home,

After embellishing a callous demeanor,
My emotions were severed,
And my heart became tough as leather,

Since your devotion continued to be absent,
My feelings for you,
Were invaded by displeasure and resentment,
       As seasons past,
       Reasons for a relationship lost its demand,
       And I renounce any reparations,
       You instigated my way,
       To petition a resolution,
              Now that I am of age,
              I have become a man of grudges,
              And a man of rage,
Because you decided to maintain distance,
The love of a father and son,
Will permanently remain nonexistent.

TRYING TO BE A MAN

Trying to understand,
What it takes to be a man,
With no plan,
No guiding hand,
        I searched for help,
        Only to be led back to myself,

Sitcoms, movies, and a child's imagination,
        Became the catalyst,
        That confirmed the persona and characteristics,
Of the man I was chasing,

        Hoping to embrace some kind of conclusion,
        To end my confusion,
I made decisions,
With no merit,
        Hoping I would inherit,
        Some type of resolution,
        To liberate myself,
From my own delusional pollution,

I pronounced myself as perfect,
        Not knowing,
I was up to my neck,
        In self-absorption and narcissism,

        I had an answer for it all,
Never realizing I would be the reason,
        For my fall,

        Now,

I sit in the middle of the floor,
With only the dark to explore,
            Grinding my teeth,
            Afraid to be speak,
            I searched for deliverance in my sleep.

SOCIETY'S WEB

Why in the hell should I play it safe?
Afraid to make a mistake,
Getting up an extra twenty minutes early,
Just so I won't be late.
      I mean damn; you only live once.
      Why should I handcuff myself with rules and regulations?
      Instead of letting go,
      And becoming submerged in my temptations,
      Not worrying about the complications.
If I could I would, but I can't,
I am a victim of society,
And most of the time I'm sleep,
While society lives for me.
Leading me to nowhere from nowhere.
      I conform to the latest trends,
      Viewing my own perceptions as foolishness,
      I dance to the rhythms of society's music,
      Unable to refuse it.
I dream of being free,
Not labeled by society and his vindictive ways,
An individual,
One who submits to my own wants and needs.
But, reality resurfaces and the chirping of society awakens me.
      With a gasp of air,
      I grin,
      Realizing there is no end to society's derangement.

SLOW DOWN

Running so fast,
You never looked both ways,
When you crashed,
Headfirst into your reckless ways.

Always chasing age,
You were overcome by his blaze.
With your eyes wide shut,
You never looked before you jumped.
Now surrounded by misfortunes and bad decisions,
With no relief in sight,
You question if your life is worth living.

Running so fast,
You never looked both ways,
When you crashed,
Headfirst into your reckless ways.

You thought lust and love were one in the same,
Persecuted and victimized for failing to know the game.
You now find your heart slain,
Corrupted by the idea of love,
Your body was disrupted by passions touch.
So quick to say yes,
Never understanding you were giving away more than just sex.
Abandon and left alone,
You must now deal with your new arrival,
On your own.

Running so fast,
You never looked both ways,

When you crashed,
Headfirst into your reckless ways.

Knocking on memories door,
Hoping to find answers to the night before.
Too much smoking and drinking,
Blurred your vision,
And altered your thinking.
And still you befriended the bottle,
And all other substances that followed.
Unaware of the decline of your weight,
Your thoughts remain cloudy,
And you've abandoned your religious faiths.
Unwilling to accept the claim that you're an addict,
The abuse of your mind and body leads you closer to your very
own casket.

TO THE SKY

Fighting the struggle,
I continue to hustle.
Doing everything I can,
To meet the world's supplies and demands.
I find,
I'm always behind,
On the constant decline.
Trying to leap every bound,
I've been shot down,
Descending to my fatal end,
Once I touched ground.

Still,
After challenging adversity,
I fell into the arms of serenity.
With my head held high,
As I look to the sky.

A lost love,
Had me searching for anonymous hugs.
Hoping to replace what I had before,
I looked behind every door,
Only to discover,
Countless lovers,
To occupy my time,
Cause you were no longer mine.
Realizing my mistake,
I find I'm too late,
After allowing my chance at love to escape.

Still,
After squandering fidelity,
I fell into the arms of serenity.
With my head held high,
As I look to the sky.

Dark Tragedies

FIRST DEGREE MURDER

Unequipped to handle day to day predicaments,
I escape life's torments,
By burying it all within,
Bordered up,
And nailed shut,

But my reality,
Embodies a consistent calamity,

I attempt to appear calm and cool,
But these four walls in this room,
Are closing in,

With each breath I take,
Suicidal thoughts slowly begin to precipitate,

As the air becomes thin
I try to pretend,
That my existence is beautiful,
And my presence is irresistible,
But beneath the sadness,
And behind the madness,
Stood a individual,
A miracle,
A being,
A reason for believing,

But in the end,
Dejection sustain,
And my call for change,
Failed to ascend,

When it was all said and done,
I rested on the floor,
Admired by no one,
United with my gun,

DEPRESSION

I have been deserted,
And abandoned by light,
Left to embrace the desolate night.
      Sheltered by my fears,
      I bathe in my tears.
Gathered under my blanket of deficiencies,
I clutch emptiness,
And dream of agony.
      My pride has been retired,
      My soul set on fire,
      And a life of failures,
      Is all I have acquired.
Far from being number one,
All that I have become,
Is the lost,
The confused,
The tormented,
And the used.
      I achieve disappointment,
      Encourage let downs,
      And chase defeat with a smile.
No longer do I find reason,
For believing,
When I have been mistreated,
Since I started breathing.
      I walk through the valley of death,
      Admiring my lost steps,
Realizing from the day I was born,
I have been ridiculed and scorn.
      Forcing me to judge my existence,
      As nothing more,

But absentminded nonsense.
Leading me to my final resting place,
Where my tortured soul can escape.

DEFEATED

Every day I struggle to survive,
I try to hide the pain in my eyes,
By looking away when others pry,
        But the drama in my life,
                Denies me the chance to veto the suffering,

I wrestle with dismay to get a three count and pin,
But my heart has lost its desire to win,

        I am restless,
        My emotions have become turbulent,
                And the light at the end of the tunnel has faded,
        Nominating it absent,
With nothing to gain,
I refrain,
                From optimism,
                By avoiding perverse antagonism,

Pronouncing myself empty and cold,
I sit alone,
Possessing my deflated soul.

LOST

Delusional thoughts kept me running reckless,
Escaping reality,
I found shelter in my dreams.

> Unable to differentiate between what's right and what's
> wrong,
> I've concocted reasons,
> That enjoy me believing,
> I don't belong.

I dispatch thoughts unkind,
Causing a commotion amongst the kind.

> Wanting to be rescued,
> I yell out,
> But no one hears me shout,
> And I realize it's my own hands covering my mouth.

Feeling worn and confused,
I sprint out of my shoes,

> Till I'm powerless to take another step,
> I swallow my last breath.
> Accepting my fate,
> Understanding intervention is too late.

Suffering the cost,
I'm left jaded, bewildered, and lost.

CONFUSION

I'm lost,
So, I search for answers within,
Praying my confusion will come to an end.
        Family and friends are no help,
        All I have is self.
Unable to make decisions,
My progression,
Stays missin.
        I show myself pity,
        By looking at my life as half full,
        Instead of being half empty.
Since I have no destination,
I find myself chasing,
A life worth wasting.
        My thoughts are always incomplete,
        My only stability,
        Is that I sleep, shit, and eat.
I've run into a wall,
I'm unable to climb,
Watching reality shows,
To occupy my time,
My habits,
Have become my crime.
        Digging myself into a hole,
        With no way out,
        I've restrained my soul,
Igniting a fire with no means of egress,
I dress my life with stress,
Inhaling my last breath,
And taken my final steps.

Now crooked I stand,
Corrupted by my own hands.
Confusion waits ahead with a smile,
Prepared to spin me round,
Till I'm completely bewildered,
And my cries for help,
Go absent without a sound. (Are removed from sound)

OBSESSED

Like a moth to a flame,
You were the cause of my pain.
            Corrupted with the misery,
            That had me believing destiny was meant for you
            and me,
      My imagination took me on a ride,
      And my volition was eradicated,
      By my emotions breaking free from inside,
I pushed my sanity out the door,
For what my infatuation adores,
            I'm fully aware this is wrong,
            But my delusional heart tells me with you is
            where I belong,
      When alone,
      My jealousy explodes,
      And I become distant and cold,
Misguided by my emotions,
And a false hope of devotion,
            I'm unfit to establish if this love is real,
            And if the way I feel,
            Should be liberated and revealed,
      As the walls close in,
      My desires are tormented,
      By the determined epidemic,
      Of passion detonating from within,
I don't know how much longer I can suppress and restrict,
These feelings that are creating subliminal conflicts,
            As the tide in my eyes,
            Begin to rise,
            I realize I've eluded my mind,

Painfully I force myself to sleep,
Where I can congregate with dreams,
That pacifies the souls of the lonely and the weak.

DEATH UNHEARD

I lay on my back,
With strangers standing over me,
Staring at disbelief.
Watching their lips move,
At a rate that's bewildering,
I find sound not to be available.
Scores of fingers pointing blame,
While eyes tense and scatter with each frantic look at my face,
Truth is being lost.
Crying out for answers,
I alarmingly go unheard,
Leaving me disturbed and wondering.
Counting the drops of rain bounce off the pavement,
Realizing reaction to touch is no longer granted,
And those once huddled over me now missing.

Drug Influence

CANDYMAN

From sunup to sundown,
Alleyways and street corners become my playground.
        Making my living,
        Off sinful desires and people's addictions.
        It is really not hard to figure out,
        Money, truly is what it is all about,
        Shit,
        I am the neighborhood candyman,
        And I do all I can,
        To meet your demands.
        Providing treats to satisfy all your needs,
        You'll be on your hands and knees praying, worrying me
        please,
        Willing to do anything,
        Reaching far and beyond the normal realm of sanity,
        Just for a sample of my candy.
And on the 1st and 15th,
You come running to me.
        With hand in pocket, full of green,
        Neglecting all responsibilities,
        You hand it all over to me.
        Knowing I'll give you all you deserve,
        Sending you on a first-class trip,
        To a point of no return.
Yet there are a reluctant few,
On an impossible mission,
Trying to fight their addiction,
Running around like headless chickens,
Shaken and twitchen.
        But, even those that ambitiously stray,
        Find their way,

Back in my arms,
Begging for a taste.
Eventually strung out, they fall,
Wondering aimlessly,
Through the sleepless night and sinful smog.
Like a Shepard leading his sheep,
When I call,
They come to me faithfully,
In this city of Babylon,
I am God!

HEROIN

Do not call it a comeback,
      I have been here for years,

Pumping my love into your veins,
Filling your heart with my pain,
I took you for a ride on tragedies train,

A lost soul is what you became,
      When the clouds denied the sun,
And addiction covered you in its shade,

Unable to recognize your own reflection,
Deception,
Has injected a false conception,
      Having you believe,
      A nonexistent fantasy,
      When in reality,
        You embraced,
      A destructive flame,
        That burns the sensible,
      And ignites the insane,

I am more than anyone can handle,
      It is said I am a magician,
The way I transform lives to shambles,
From just one sample,

You cannot escape this feeling,
That is intoxicating and appealing

I did not make the rules,
       I just play the game,
And pursue,
          The weak
     The forgotten,
          And the lost,
          Some say I am ruff, rugged, and raw,

I say,
       I am all the above and more,
       Everything you adore,
       And all your desires to explore,

I am the medication prescribed,
       Those feelings erupting inside,
A disturbance you cannot describe,
       An infatuation you dare not deny,

Together until the end,
       Forever I am,
Your friend,
Heroin.

STRUNG-OUT

In search of true love and affection,
I found a world of misfortune and drugs,
Becoming just another slave,
To its kisses and hugs.

     Hypnotize by its eyes,
     I saw more lows than highs.
     Willing to cheat, deceive, and lie,
     I did whatever to get high,
     Even if it meant giving away my body,
     To any, and everybody.

There was no shame,
No pain,
No reason to explain,
No one to place blame,
For the beast within I could not tame.

     Weather had no bearing on my soul,
     I would walk the streets,
     Enduring the rain, sleet, and snow.
     Never to ignore a chance to score,
     I would drop to all four's,
     To satisfy what my mind and body adores.

Blind to see,
What my conscious was afraid to believe,

     I had one mission
     One goal,
     One decision

Everything else was frivolous,
To my burning addictions happiness.

My nights were endless,
Walking alongside Satan,
Never was it hard to tell,
Or too complicated to spell,
I was now in Hell.

Unaware of my whereabouts,
Disregarding all who tried to reach out,
I lay in the filth,
Of my own destruction,
Bled dry and strung-out.

Damaged Goods

DAMAGED GOODS

A beautiful sight,
Under Hell's light, (under a strobe/flickering light)
I held tight,
As you lead me through,
The hallways of your life.
       You introduced me,
       To pain and agony,
       And your childhood friend misery.
While exposing me to cruelty,
You open my heart,
To a damaged soul's reality.
       In plain view and unscripted,
       I was allowed in,
       Where others were not before permitted.
Unlocking the doors,
To horrors,
That made me question moving forward.
       I went along for the ride,
       Knowing the terrors erupting inside.
Devastation scolded my eyes,
While my screams were drowned out,
By the silence of cries.
       Bearing a grin,
       Tasteful as sin,
I believed I could make a difference,
Enduring what many would have not forgiven.

Bedeviled by your words,
I followed you to the infernal,
Where devastation is delivered and served,
Never took the time,
To materialize,
If your doctrines were organized,
My uncalculated decisions became the crime,
That governed my demise,
I assumed you had the answers to my questions,
But in the end, I realize I was asking the wrong questions,
You were the unsolved butchery,
That asphyxiated my creativity,
And took custody of my humanity,
You intentionally bewildered my soul,
Leaving my psyche puzzled,
And my spirit baffled,
Forcing the grip on my rationale to fold,
I thought you were a blessing,
A modern-day miracle,
But all I was shown,
Were false lessons,
That centered me in a present-day crucible,
Everyone on the outside,
Assumed I lost my mind,
When I couldn't make since,
Of my predicament,
Never discovered,
By no other,
You became an apparition,
Of my animated and vivid supposition,

Eventually I was chastised,
And crucified,
For believing your lies.

A MUTILATED HEART

Your deceptive web of lies,
Led to my demise,
My descent began,
When I welcomed your hand,
Your allure captivated and mesmerized,
When I should have been terrified,
By the devastation you left behind,
From the tortured and victimized,
Blinded by your beautiful sight,
You depleted my heart,
When you took a chunk out of my conscience,
And ripped my emotions apart,
I could not apprehend the signs,
When love took me up so high,
That it took years for me to come down,
And accept reality with both feet on the ground,
With the destruction of my soul,
My sanity chose to let go,
Leaving me bewildered and wondering about,
Unconcern with my route,
I pursued a false belief,
That led me to the heart of cheat,
After failing numerous times,
Trying to capture the divine,
My love for you,
Clashed with my will to survive,
And still,
My feelings were not willing to resign,
I've become an all-inclusive mess,

Blanketed by stress,
    Governed astray,
    By a legend in the game,
You sucked me in,
And decimated my nature,
For adoring your trends.

DENIAL

With nothing more but, a wave of the hand,
A tear in my eye,
And a reluctant goodbye.
I watched you walk out of my life.

Searching for the reasons why,
You and I could not give this one more try.

I was unwilling to accept the claim,
That the whisper of others was to blame
When it was you and I,
Who extinguished our loves burning flame.

With the loss of you,
The edge is near,
And I find myself submerged in my fears.

I pinch myself,
Hoping I'll wake from this horrific dream,
But, what I'd hope to be a dream,
I find to be a broken hearts reality.

I can't handle this,
I'm getting desperate,
Counting down the days, hours, and minutes.

When you left,
You took the stride from my step,
My ability to unconditionally accept,
As well as my natures breath.

There was only you,
And nothing else.
Disrobing my heart,
And diminishing an attitude that was nonchalant.

Bewildered and confused,
I refuse the screaming update of breaking news,
Of you turning down the side streets,
Into the arms of another dude.

My heart won't accept,
What my eyes have found to be true.
And why should it,
When for 9 years,
Everything was you.

Cold and lonely,
I don't have a clue on what to do.
Uninhibited by my surroundings,
I'm forced to realize,
There is no more me and you.

JEZEBEL

43

Unattainable like the wind,
You spun me round and round,
Confused and trippin.

    Chasing the fascination of maybe,
    Embracing the suspicion of you and me.

You lead and I followed,
Dragging me through,
Empty days,
Wasteful nights,
And nowhere tomorrows.

    Still, I was caught,
    Restrain by your essence,
    And detained by your presence.

I laid down when you walked,
And swallowed my opinions when you talked.

    You were my everything,
    My dreams,
    My fantasies,
    All the things and more,
    I imagine you to be.

Unconcerned with your ways,
That induced past hearts astray.

    I push to the rear your lies,
    And brought forward the reasons why,
    It should forever be you and I.

Yet you carried on for seasons,
With no reasons, for your treason,
Along with a love misleading,
Tearing my heart apart,
Leaving me breathless and bleeding.

Nevertheless, I was a prisoner in your storm,
        Of neglection and deception,
        Becoming a victim of hearts torn.

Unaware of the ringing alarm,
You brought harm,
To all that I am,
Suspended lifeless in your arms.

        Never did I care,
        Whether you were here or there,
        When no one can compare.

You are my burning flame,
As well as my hearts pain,
Driving me insane,
Unable to take one breath,
Without mentioning your name.

TAKEN FOR A RIDE

You have brought me to where the oppressed congregate,
And the tortured migrate,

I was a fool to believe,
In you and me,

Your innocent disposition,
Kept hidden,
Your true intentions,

Keeping me unaware,
Of the false care,
You provided throughout this affair,

With each heart clinching blow,
I came close to deserting my soul,

Believing with you I begin,
I did not comprehend,
You would be my end,

Your smile mesmerized,
Your words hypnotized,
And your touch paralyzed,

I was left bewildered and emotionless,

Your appeal,
Tainting everything that was real,

I found myself struck,
By the hands that corrupt,
>When I went for a ride,
>>With the promise of love,
>>Employing kisses and hugs,
>>>Instead, I was manipulated,
>By loving eyes,
That fed me to heartbreaks and homicide.

Why am I here?
Conversation have been deserted,
     Happiness and anger have switched roles,
Leaving behind,
     Two empty souls,
     Comforted by the desolate cold,
And adopted by the seclusion of fear,

Why do I stay?
     You have told me numerous times,
     You no longer appreciate my kind,
       And still I hang around,
Willingly knowing,
Your destructive words,
Take pleasure in,
     Holding me down,
Defeating my confidence,
     With the slightest utter of your sounds,
I try to separate,
From your persuading familiarity,
I devoutly chase,
But,
My audacity arrived too late,

Why can't I leave?
     Unable to say goodbye,
     I rely,
On my diluted imagination,
Forever embracing,
A situation,
     That involves your touch,

Never determining,
I would be asking too much,
             I acquired,
             A false desire,
That compelled me to believe,
That you were fascinated with me,

My heart is weak,
Thoughts are incomplete,
         And everywhere I turn,
It is your image I see,

Every night I close my eyes,
And fantasize,
         Tomorrow morning,
Will discover you by my side,

         Where have you gone,
         What did I do wrong,
Why do you feel,
         You know longer belong,

When you left,
         You walked away with the spark,
         That generated life for my heart,
And existence to my breath,

I have surrendered myself to an emotional disaster,
Verbally abusing my character,
         Praying you would hear,
         As each tear,
         Fled my eyes,
         Abducting my desire to survive,
         But you ignored my cry,
And now,
         I no longer can celebrate days,
         That do not include you and I,

Abandoned with a devalued soul,
I am compelled to let go,
        With you missing from my life,
My world has become,
        A menacing sight,
        Of toxic strife.

Holding On

BEWILDERED HEART

Searching, no longer traveling a path of love,
That has been misleading.
Reality has given pardon to my heart,
And now life must go on.

Avoiding the side streets of misery.
Unwilling to dwell in the alleyways of pain,
I've found disparity to be comforting,
But still the taste of blissful love my heart quenches.

Even though being alone brings peace of mind,
To love creates a passage of eternal happiness.

Only the identity of true love is permanent and unchanging

BARELY HOLDING ON

I feel torn and incomplete,
And during the stillness of the night, I weep.

Frustrated with being alone,
I try to get a hold,
On my dwindling soul,
But pain forces me to let go.

A witness to my own fate,
The rising of the sun,
Has shed light on my mistakes,
Bringing truth to light,
Reality has imprisoned my sight,
Demanding I don't look away.

I find myself,
Traveling down a bottomless hole,
Where I have abandoned my spirit,
Along with my hope,
Leaving me in the comforts of my tears,
And the cold.

Left to suffer on my own,
I question my will,
By swallowing scores of pills,
Praying I'll find my way home.

And still, I've maintained,
After the struggles,
The troubles,
And countless attempts,
I've remained.

DO YOU REMEMBER

When you left,
Did my name escape your breath?
      By chance,
      Do you close your eyes?
      And let thoughts of us,
      Travel through your mind.
Do you dream of me?
When you're sleep,
Or have I become a forgotten memory?
      Has my image drifted so far into the night,
      That it has evaded your sight.
Can you remember the goofy laughter?
And the trivial chit-chatter.
      Remember the arguing, the fights,
      And how we made-up all night.
What about the private talks,
And confidential long walks.
      Do you think back to those days,
      When everything stood still,
      And unconcerned we laid,
      With nothing but time to kill.
Can you recall the love letters?
And how we both said,
This would last forever.
      And how bout all those sweet nothins,
      Deafening our ears,
      About how we would conquer each other's fears.
I can remember it all,
That's why I still call,

STAYING TOGETHER

Undesirable is how I feel when you come around,
In your absence,
Silence becomes a delightful sound.
      Neither one of us has the courage to leave,
            When we both agree,
            We no longer believe,
      The two of us were meant to be.
In a room of four walls,
Distance is all we share,
Annoyed by one another,
Wishing the other wasn't there.
      But still, we both remain,
            Unable to explain,
      When we both feel the same.
We're equally agitated by each other's presence,
Yet no one makes an exit.
      You say it's me,
            I say it's you,
            But in reality,
      Neither one of us has a clue.
As the year ends,
And a new one begins,
We find ourselves at the others throat again.
      Understanding we're a mess,
            We both confess,
            Staying together,
      Is causing us two unwanted stress.
So, you go your way,
And I go mine,
But with time,
Nor you or I,

Can deny,
How empty we feel without the other by our side.
        Now back together,
                After enduring disastrous weather.
With a newfound appreciation,
For a love no longer depreciating,
We now find worth celebrating.

Self-Discovery—The Painful Truth

I CAN

I can,
        Break the chain,
        And escape the stain,
        That has corrupted,
        The identity of generations before,
        Who sustained,
        And maintained,
        For the day,
        I could succeed,
        And achieve,
        Overcoming time's test,
        That laid my forefathers to rest,
                I can,
                        Say yes to change,
                        And open my arms,
                        To embrace the blame,
                        For societies screaming alarm,
                        When turbulence is created,
                        By one debated,
                        To be the most hated,
                        For the revolution,
                        That has emerged
                        To amend,
                        Our present sins,
I can,
        Stand alone,
        In a country far from my own,
        And fight,
        For the right,
        To have a democracy,
        Not shadowed by hypocrisy,

In a land,
I now call home,
        I can,
                Be a witness,
                To the existence,
                Of greatness,
                Identified,
                And lead a diverse group of people,
                To the promise land,
                Where all stands,
                United and undivided,

FALSE DEPICTION

I mask,
Conceal,
And disguise,
What is going on behind these brown eyes.
       Unwilling to allow anyone into my domain,
       With the fear of them discovering,
       I am uncomplicated and plain.
So, I reside neighboring an existence of pretend,
Keeping my true identity hidden.
I continue to present myself in a different light,
Fighting off certainty,
With an explosion of lies,
Creating my own reality.
       Hoping to be appreciated for something I am not,
       I cannot stop,
       Pinning the trigger down,
       I shoot lies endlessly,
       Until the truth can no longer be found.
And all that is left,
Are the false steps,
I have composed,
To become the person, I want to expose.

I devoured my mistakes,
And acknowledge my fate,
      Appreciating perfection to be fantasy,
      And inaccuracies to be reality.
I am able to push ahead,
Emerging myself from the thankless dead.
      Understanding blessings are being earned,
      With each lesson learn,
      Unafraid of being burn,
      I am willing to receive my turn.
Respecting the foul smell,
That leads innocence to Hell.
      I am fully aware of what I do not know,
      And what I need to know.
I recognize being wrong,
Is sometimes where I belong.
      And at times creeping with night,
      Instead of bearing strong with light.
Tolerating my good and my bad,
Here before you I stand.

FINDING MY WAY

I need to get away,
In search of a new day.
Where serenity is inevitable,
And words of destruction are unthinkable.

    I long to walk strong beside assurance,
    Stepping out of a world of hypocritical nonsense.

Realizing my wealth,
In the truth of myself,
Knowing that others acceptance,
Holds no importance.

    Until I know who I am inside and out,
    Unconcerned over surrounding doubts,
    Just cause my path,
    May not be the popular route.

And I've found,
After abandoning all the negative sounds,
That I no longer allowed anymore,
Was what laid behind my hearts very own door.

    Was my very own way,
    To my new day,
    Where I can escape and play,

And life's simplicities,
Are not tainted by societies hypocrisy.

SPREAD MY WINGS

I'm going to spread my wings and fly,
High above my worries,
Unconcerned with ages of negative memories.
Shedding my layers of grudges and heartaches.
Swallowing the answer pill,
Relieving me of life's headaches.
Putting a strangle hold on day-to-day pains,
Avoiding society's side streets, alleyways, and fast lanes.
No longer will I be led a stray,
By the illusion of waiting for tomorrow,
What I can have today.

I'm going to spread my wings and fly,
High above envy,
And deceptions alluring eye.
Locking up my wrongful pleasures.
Throwing away the key,
Releasing my soul,
Setting my faith free.
Making my way out of the dark,
Into the light,
From being once blind,
To now having sight.
No more am I a victim of my immoral ways,
I now move violently along the Lord's path,
With a burning blaze.

I'm going to spread my wings and fly,
High above my torn heart,
And questions of why.
Soaring over sunken relationships,

Waving goodbye to its troubles and bullshit.
Spending my time being productive,
Shying from the cravings of lust and seduction.
Getting myself together,
Knowing that I can do better.
Instead of wasting my time,
Searching for what only,
My heart can find.

I'm going to spread my wings and fly,
High above,
Traveling with exuberance,
Alongside happiness.
Touching ground in jubilation,
Just outside of exhilaration.
Finally shaken hands with prosperity,
After being embraced by vivacity.
With the realism,
That my life is outlined by optimism.

THE INFORMANT

You conquered land,
With just the wave of a hand,
Still, I'm criticized for wanting to be treated like a man.
One who is your equal,
Instead of what lies beneath you.
Just because I speak my mind,
Unlike the others whose thoughts run and hide.
I cannot do that,
I must deliver the facts.
And break through the wax of lies,
That has tainted my people ears,
For hundreds of years.
Shining light on the truth,
For today's starving youth,
Stripped of our culture, our beliefs, and our accomplishments,
We were sold,
On what we were told.
The schools kept hidden,
Our true beginnings.
Having us believe we were less of a man,
While all along we were the original man.
Placing shackles on our minds,
And binders on our eyes.
We knew only what you told us,
And saw only what you showed us.
Unaware we were royalty,
Men were kings,
And women were queens.
We were using mathematics to configure and build,
And communicated with language,
While they all lived in caves and grunted like savages.

And still we were chosen to be damaged,
Giving a life of disadvantages,
And told to manage,
Overwhelming challenges.
Now you're so surprised,
That we survived.
Trying to act like you're ashamed,
For treating us like animals needing to be tamed.
While along in your mind,
You wish we could go back in time,
To those days when you ruled our minds.
That's why I must awaken my young brothers and sisters sleeping,
And give them the teachings.
Releasing them from the deceitful dark,
Leading them to the light of truth,
Giving their life a new spark.

Love, Women,

and Relationships/Pleasure & Ecstasy

SABLE

Chocolate sky,
Blackberry rain,
Drip down on my nature,
And touch my soul.

My mahogany sun,
Shine your rays of ebony,
And breathe life into all.

Auburn hills, copper mountains, chestnut waterfalls,
And shores radiate with waves of brown sugar,
Smashing onto its hazel sand.

Falling stars leave scares of scintillating cinnamon,
Across the sky.
Truth has been found,
Sable you are sublime.

TO LOVE YOU

I want to indulge your bodies craving rapture.
I want to embrace you,
       Touch you,
       Caress you,
Life with you is all I want.

I want to taunt your mind, with thoughts of euphoria.
I want to entice you,
       Obsess you,
       Infatuate you,
To desire you is all I want.

I want to submit to your natures undivided needs.
I want to befriend you,
       Arouse you,
       Thrill you,
To complete you is all I want.

A WOMAN'S ESSENCE

Life follows in your path.
Days are optimistic when you laugh.
Chasing elation captured by your smile,
With love that stretches further than a mile.
Sensual desires erupt with your presence.
Woman you are the reason for my existence.
Dreams rupture with images of you.
A serene cool is what you exude.
Just as the rising of the sun,
You awake life into all.
You are times pick-me-up when he falls.
You are man's beginning and his end.
You are days without sin.
You open and close all doors.
You are the nucleus of evolutions core.
Woman I thank you.
You are beyond remarkable,
Forever radiant.
For you are justly in the groove.

EVERYTHING I IMAGINE YOU TO BE

Unable to utter a sound,
When you are around.
    Your presence is breath taking,
    Leaving me shaking,
    When I think about your love,
    That is undeniably amazing.
Everything and more,
Is what you bring through the door.

Whenever I envision love making,
There is no mistaking,
It is you I want for the taking.
    You are an infatuation of lust,
    Others desire to touch.
With a smile,
That drives all in a crowd wild.

Your appeal is so intoxicating.
    That sometimes I feel,
    This cannot be real.
But I am reassured by your kiss,
Every time,
Are lips combine.

You make me believe,
I can do anything,
So, to your heart I sing,
Out of tone and terribly off key.
    And unaware of any notes,
    Cause I do not care,
If I am the center of everyone's jokes.

You are my one chance at romance.
> And I hope you will take my hand,
> Honoring me as your man.
Together with our hearts dangerously united,
Along with our souls recklessly binded.

Sickened, stressed, alone,
I cannot make it on my own,
Without you I have no home.
        What more can I say,
        You are on my mind,
        Every minute,
        And every hour,
        Of every day,
On bended knee I give to you,
My heart to forever be true.
        My life now has meaning,
        And because of you,
        Seeing is believing,
You ignite an eruption I cannot tame,
I have no shame,
To lay by your side,
I will endure all types of pain.
        Aroused by your touch,
        I crave for your clutch,
        For your body,
        I can never have enough.
With every breath I take,
I shed all my mistakes,
To take the chance of losing your love,
Is far too great,
        Because of you my dreams have come true,
        Now all I do,
        I do,
        Because of you.
Whether it is raining, sleeting, or snowing,
You must know,
I will never let you go,

This I vow,
With my mind, body, and soul.

A TRIBUTE TO YOU

I appreciate all that you are,
For adoring my faults,
As well as my assets.

You are appreciated for being the one woman,
Who stands by me,
Keeping my character intact,
When others slaughter my name with fictitious lies,
Demoralizing my caliber.

I appreciate your patience,
When understanding my stubborn reasoning,
And childish justification of my wrong doings.

You are appreciated for your zealous warmth,
That embraces my dismal heart.

Cherished, adulated, admired, treasured,
Honored, and respected.
Still no amount of words,
Can testify the woman you are to me.

MY THIRST FOR WOMEN

To feed my desires,
I was willing to step into the fire.
Searching for what my body adored,
I repeatedly went back for more.
  Disrupting what I have at home,
  I was corrupted,
  By the streets I roamed.
Unwilling to face the music,
I continued to abuse it.
Assuming she'll never find out,
What I'm truly about.
  I've tried to domesticate,
  My lustful taste,
  And bring an end,
  To my adulterous trends,
But to many options makes it hard,
When you have a love for fast cars.
  There walk,
  There scent,
  There smile,
  Drives me wild.
Stopping me cold in my tracks,
Forcing me to react.
  To what I know is wrong,
  But just like hook, line, and sinker,
  They pull me along.
Making it improper for me to begin,
To try and find my peace within,
Which appears I've abandoned,
By choosing to live,
A life of sin.

I have an appetite,
I decline to fight.
Refusing to turn on the lights,
I relish the night.

TONIGHT

Tonight,
I will inspire you with my touch,
Arouse you with my stroke,
And corrupt your innocence,
Till your body screams enough,

Tonight,
The sounds of words are stolen,
Only the peaceful bliss of your bodies cry,
And angelic moaning,
Are allowed to be spoken,

Tonight,
You will be,
Embraced by my ecstasy,
And I will answer all your desires,
Provoking your natures fire,
And together we will satisfy,
One another's fantasies,

Tonight,
We will eclipse all nights before,
And encounter a passionate force,
Creating a spark,
From the excitement of two hearts,
After penetrating infatuations core.

ALL I WANNA DO   79

I wanna lie beside you,
Fondle your hair,
Caress your skin,
Corrupt your nature with my lips.

I wanna take your hand,
Stair into your eyes,
Whisper seductive melodies in your ear,
Lose control from the intoxication of your scent.

I wanna grab hold of your body,
Pull you near,
Send you on a voyage,
Fulfilling your fantasies,
Taken you round and round,
Leaving you shaken and spent.

I wanna ignite your juices,
Taste your passion,
Escape into your dreams,
Chasing your emotions,
Quivering after each kiss.

I wanna wake-up next to you,
Consumed by morning breath,
And matted hair,
With no reason to care,
Enjoying the morning after,
And all its foolishness.

LOVE

You are my desires,
          My true intentions,
          My reason for living,
You are my eternal fire.

You are the sparkle in my eyes,
          The core of my soul,
          A feeling untold,
You are the rapture my heart cries.

You are ecstasy found to be awake,
          The scent of passion,
          The frontier of obsession,
You are infatuation to be craved.

          You are my all,
          You are my everything,
          Love is who you are.

Random Thoughts

REVIVED

With a shot in the dark,
You created a spark,
And ignited my heart.
Giving life to a once dejected soul,
That was tossed aside and discarded to suffer alone.

ALLURING EYES

Drugged by a look,
Unimagined by words.
My soul is inspired,
By your glare.
Silent I stand,
Unable to move.
Desires aroused,
Encounters visions of life,
Through your eyes.
With a stare that has,
Captured my essence.
Helpless to my surprise,
I have fallen victim.

JEHOVAH

When you were falling,
Pride denounced my support,
And still I kept calling,
Unwilling to surrender my hand,
I will not give up,
Until you're able to stand.

WHAT IF? 85

What if misery and pain were not the contents of my life?
Would the dream of everlasting happiness still remain absent?

What if life was no longer a question?
And day-by-day living now unstable became consistent.

What if I emerged my innermost thoughts?
Would any if not all still stand.

What if hatred and sin were diminished?
Could peace and solitude now be perfected?

What if god was found to be 2 consonants and a vowel?
Would society recreate beliefs to soak their faith upon?

What if trust was truly defined?
And deception was put to rest.

What if guaranteed was able for all,
Would money be burned as a proposed source of heat?

PERPETRATOR

You proclaim your fame,
In a well composed masterpiece,
Orchestrated by corrupted truths,
And masked deceit.
    Your very existence is described,
    By a chain of lies.
Coming straight out of a comic book,
With your misleading looks.

Invest past the stain of my skin.
I think, understand, comprehend, dictate, and opinionate.
I won't change my value.
Why be afraid?
We are one in the same,
Still, all I feel is pain.
Your eyes picture fear,
When they shoot me.
Complete hypocrisy impregnates your mind,
Determined only by my cast,
I die in the first take.
No longer will your passive smile,
Hide your atrocious eye.
I cannot be denied.
I am an individual,
A being,
An entity,
I am people of you.

AMERICA

She's a bitch,
And she knows it,
Not afraid to show it.
Her actions are explosive.

www.ingramcontent.com/pod-product-compliance
Lightning Source LLC
Chambersburg PA
CBHW070737030726
47601CB00001B/48